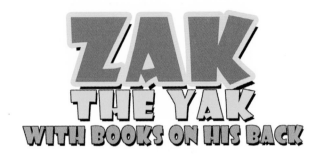

ZAK
THE YAK
WITH BOOKS ON HIS BACK

Written by

John Wood

Illustrated by

Abin Shrestha

Room to Read®

Namaste!

Zak the Yak with Books on His Back was conceived by John Wood, the founder of Room to Read, as a way to celebrate the ten-year anniversary of Room to Read. It also commemorates the opening of Room to Read's 10,000th library. Room to Read was started because the headmaster in Bahundanda asked for help. In this book we return to the place where it all began.

John was very impressed with Abin Shrestha's prior work on Room to Read's Local Language Publishing program (see page 45) and since John wanted a Nepali artist to bring Zak to life, the collaboration was born.

By promoting this book, you are helping us to load more (metaphorical) yaks with books to bring to children in remote and resource-deprived parts of the world. We hope that young students who want to help more children to gain the lifelong gift of education and literacy will join our Yak Pack (www.zaktheyak.org) and will learn more about the Students Helping Students program, featured on our website at w w w . r o o m t o r e a d . o r g .

John Wood's first book, Leaving Microsoft to Change the World, can be ordered through Amazon or Better World Books and can also be viewed at www.leavingmicrosoftbook.com. To request John as a speaker at an event, please visit www.johnwoodspeaks.com.

No yaks were harmed in the making of this epic tale.

Enjoy!

Special thanks to our friends at Scholastic for their advice and support.

Copyright © 2010 by John Wood

Project Editor: Jill Carlson

ISBN-10: 0983041709
ISBN-13: 9780983041702

Printed and bound in the USA

In the land of Nepal,
The hills are so high
That the snow-covered peaks
Almost block out the sky.

The view is so stunning.
You will stare for hours.
These mountains, it is said,
Have magical powers.

But living is tough
Up here in the hills.
Howling winds and cold weather
Cause bone-numbing chills.

The peaks are so steep,
And the rivers so wide,
That a very short journey
Can mean a very long ride.

A ride on a donkey,
Or perhaps a big yak?
For a land without roads,
Is a land made for Zak.

"Who is Zak?" you may cry,
With ear-piercing clatter.
"And what is a yak?"
"And why do they matter?"

Yaks are very big beasts,
With horns oh so long.
They thrive in high places,
And have legs that are strong.

As for Zak, well this yak,
He is one of a kind,
With a big friendly smile
And a razor-sharp mind.

He climbs high mountain passes
With big heavy loads.
He is not at all worried
That Nepal has few roads.

At each mountain village
They know him by name.
For a yak who can talk,
Is destined for fame.

He loves to drink tea
While enjoying the view.
He talks to the locals
To find out what's new.

Up high in the mountains
Was a town Zak was fond-a.
He loved every visit
To stunning Bahundanda.

On a warm spring day,
He was asked to sit down
By the local headmaster
Whose face wore a frown.

As the headmaster chatted,
Zak learned a sad tale.
"We want to run a great school,
But each day we fail."

"Our students, so many
But our books, oh so few.
We want them to learn,
But what can we do?"

"This is so wrong," said Zak.
"There's such a great need.
And every child who wants to
Should be able to read."

16

"But our village is poor,
Our resources near zero.
If you could help us change this
You'd be such a hero!"

"I'd love to," said Zak.
His face lit with a smile.
"For the sake of these students,
I'd walk many a mile."

"We'll find people to help us,
Who want life to be fair.
When they hear of our students,
They'll be willing to share."

"We'll send hundreds of emails
To build excitement and hype.
I just hope that these hooves
Will allow me to type!"

"You'll need help in the city
To get the job done.
As your special assistants,
Meet my daughter and son."

"Arul just turned twelve.
He's a hard-working lad.
His devotion to studies
Makes me a proud dad."

"A friendly young girl,
Little Manju is ten.
She will help you collect
Rupees, dollars and yen."

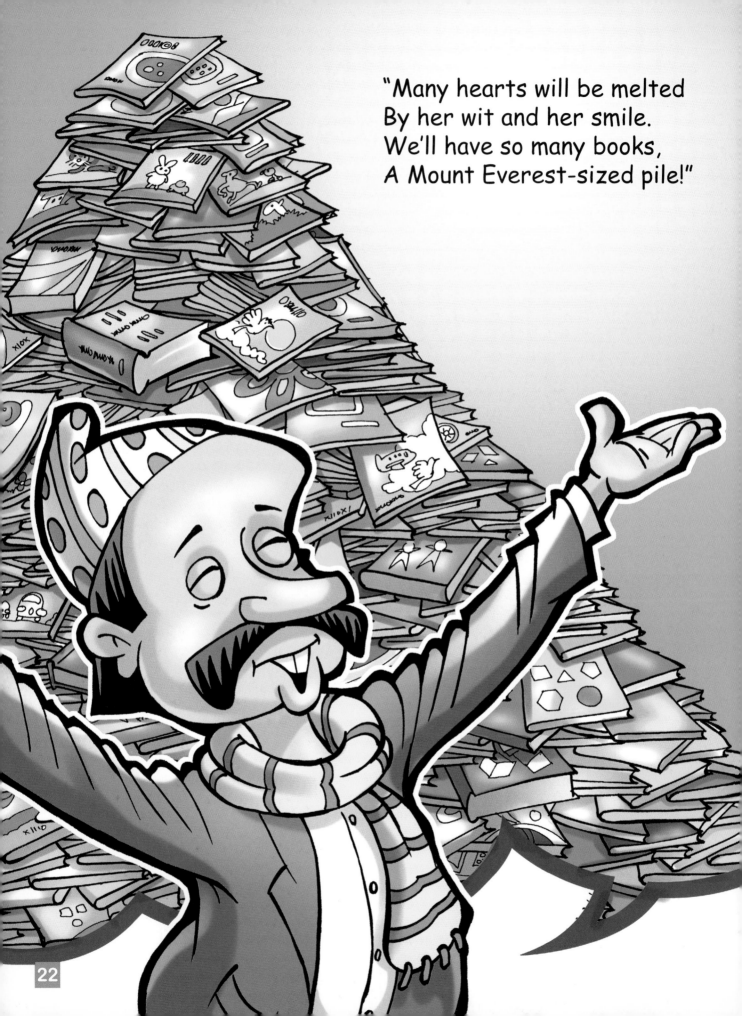

"Many hearts will be melted
By her wit and her smile.
We'll have so many books,
A Mount Everest-sized pile!"

"Let's get moving!" yelled Zak,
Who broke into a run.
"For the sooner we start
Then the sooner we're done!"

Our three heroes, they walked
Up and down the long trail.
They marched on despite
Icy winds, rain and hail.

"Yak fur," said Zak,
"Is thick and quite warm.
Bundle up on my back
'Til we get through this storm."

Feeling warm, safe and snug,
They dozed off for hours.
Zak climbed hills and crossed rivers
With his stunning yak powers!

When the siblings awoke,
The land around them was flat.
They were out of the mountains
And were thankful for that!

In the distance they spied,
Through the haze and the dew,
Could it be? Yes it was!
Hooray! Yippee! Kathmandu!

"We're here," said Zak,
"For the start of the day.
We'll eat eggs, toast, and tea
And then get on our way!"

"As you slept, I made calls
On my hands-free yak phone.
There's good news," said Zak,
"We will not work alone."

"I shared our bold plans
To bring books to the mountains.
People's offers to help us
Started gushing like fountains."

"I'm so happy," said Manju,
As she gulped down her tea.
"Let's get moving. Eat faster!
We've many people to see!"

As the news got around,
The streets were alive.
Many people were inspired
To help this book drive.

After three days of visits
All across Kathmandu,
Zak was fully loaded
With books old and new.

As the stacked yak walked west,
Guess what formed? A parade!
Our heroes were escorted
By the new friends they'd made.

Up in the mountains,
Bahundanda was preparing
For the books and adventures
They soon would be sharing.

The three friends traveled
For three days and two nights.
They carried their treasure
Up, up, up to new heights.

The villagers let off
A loud and excited cry,
As the word went around
That their friends were nearby.

The students and teachers
Lined up with their flowers.
As our heroes returned,
Petals came down in showers.

The students each grabbed
A stack of colorful books.
And their faces lit up
With the happiest looks!

43

"Three big cheers for Zak,
And for Manju and Arul!
This is the best day
In the history of our school!"

Can you imagine trying to read a book in a language you don't know?

In many places in today's world, kids do not have access to books they can understand. Books are published in a language that kids do not speak or read well. Fortunately, the team at Room to Read is working to change this.

In countries like Cambodia, South Africa, and Sri Lanka, Room to Read publishes stories written and illustrated by locals for locals. That way, kids who grow up speaking a language like Tamil or Khmer can, for the first time, read stories in their mother tongue. Want to see this theory in action? Check out pages 42 and 43. The books in the students' hands are actual covers and titles published by Room to Read in Nepal.

By purchasing this copy of Zak the Yak with Books on His Back, you have helped to put more of these local language books into the hands of kids who need them most. You are sharing your love of great stories and books with kids across the world.

If you would like to learn more about Room to Read's Local Language Publishing program, please visit www.roomtoread.org.

We're the largest children's book publisher you've never heard of… unless you speak and read Nepali.

Parent and Teachers' Guide to
Zak the Yak with Books on His Back

There are many ways to use Zak the Yak's story to introduce new concepts, content, and culture to your little learner.

- Have your student make a text-to-life connection. How is their life similar to or different than Manju and Arul's lives?

- Think aloud as you read aloud. Model good reading techniques as you read aloud by saying what's on your mind. "Hmm. I wonder how many books are in that Mount Everest-sized pile…"

- Work a mini-geography lesson into your story time. Locate Nepal on a map. Discuss the similarities and differences in climate, culture, and language.

- Use the power of prediction to model good reading. Before turning the page, ask your student what they think will happen in the following pages. Compare your predictions with what actually occurred within the text.

- Work through the hard words before you begin. Before reading the book, flip through the pages and go on a vocabulary hunt with your student. Explain the meaning in advance so when you read the story together, these difficult words will have more meaning.

- Plot the elements of the story on a story map. Help your student identify the problem, specific events, and the solution.

- Use Zak to practice phonemic awareness. List words that rhyme with Zak the Yak, Arul (ah-ROOL), and Manju (MAHN-joo). Orally segment the word Bahundanda (BAH-hoon-don-duh) and practice speaking multisyllabic words.

- Describe the characters in the book. List the traits and characteristics of Zak, the headmaster, the villagers, Manju, and Arul.

- Make use of the beautiful illustrations to teach about setting. Ask your student to name two different places the story takes place (Bahundanda and Kathmandu). Discuss how they are similar and different.

- Split up the story elements and have your student order them. Write the events in the story on cards, and help your student sequence them in order.

- Identify causes and effects in the story. Review the story elements and discuss what resulted when Zak, Manju, and Arul committed to helping Bahundanda.

Room to Read®

Author:

John Wood

John Wood is the Founder and Board Chair of Room to Read. He grew up in a family that loved books and reading, and with access to a local library. So when a headmaster in Nepal showed him an empty library, and over 400 students who wanted to learn to read, it was only natural that he would try to help them. John eventually returned to the village of Bahundanda with thousands of books, and shortly thereafter quit his executive position with Microsoft to start Room to Read. Zak the Yak with Books on His Back was written to celebrate the ten-year anniversary of Room to Read in 2010. The book salutes the organization's humble beginnings, while also celebrating the opening of our 10,000th Reading Room (library). Over four million children like Arul and Manju now have access to Room to Read's libraries across nine countries in Africa and Asia.

Illustrator:

Abin Shrestha

Abin Shrestha is a well-known cartoonist in Nepal. Thousands of his cartoons have been featured in a variety of publications and Abin has earned honors and recognition for his work. He recently published a book of his work entitled, Abin's Cartoon Collection Part One. Abin also illustrates comic strips and children's book and he has been a prominent illustrator in Room to Read's Local Language Publishing program. He graduated with a degree in Fine Arts from Tribhuvan University in Nepal and he currently works as a senior cartoonist at Kantipur Publications. To see more of his work, please visit http://www.abin.com.np/.

Zak loves to travel to see new places and meet new friends. Copy this Zak, cut him out, and take him on adventures! If you would like Zak to see places far from your home, mail Zak to friends and family and ask them to take him on adventures too! Learn more about Zak and play yak-tastic games at www.zaktheyak.org.

Room to Read®